FLIGHT OF THE

HUMMINGBIRD

MICHAEL NICOLL YAHGULANAAS

with Wangari Maathai and
His Holiness the Dalai Lama

FLIGHT OF THE

HUMMINGBIRD

A PARABLE FOR THE ENVIRONMENT

GREYSTONE BOOKS

Douglas & McIntyre Publishing Group

Vancouver/Toronto/Berkeley

08 09 10 11 12   5 4 3 2 1

Greystone Books
A division of Douglas & McIntyre Ltd.
2323 Quebec Street, Suite 201
Vancouver, British Columbia
Canada V5T 4S7
www.greystonebooks.com

Library and Archives Canada Cataloguing in Publication
Yahgulanaas, Michael Nicoll
Flight of the hummingbird / artwork by Michael Nicoll Yahgulanaas ;
essays by Wangari Maathai and His Holiness the Dalai Lama.

ISBN 978-1-55365-372-1

1. Environmental protection in art. 2. Hummingbirds in art.
3. Parables in art. 4. Environmental protection—Citizen participation.
5. Environmental responsibility. 6. Environmental protection—Folklore.
7. Hummingbirds—Folklore. 8. Quechua Indians—Folklore.
I. Maathai, Wangari II. Bstan-´dzin-rgya-mtsho, Dalai Lama XIV, 1935− III. Title.
ND249.Y34F56 2008   759.11   C2007-905922-8

Editing by Michelle Benjamin
Copy editing by Wendy Fitzgibbons
Jacket and text design by Jessica Sullivan
Printed and bound in Canada by Friesens
Printed on paper that does not contain
materials from trees of old-growth forests.
Distributed in the U.S. by Publishers Group West

We gratefully acknowledge the financial support of the Canada Council for the
Arts, the British Columbia Arts Council, the Province of British Columbia through
the Book Publishing Tax Credit, and the Government of Canada through the Book
Publishing Industry Development Program (BPIDP) for our publishing activities.

For Tsuaay & LR in appreciation

CONTENTS

Wangari Maathai

WISDOM OF THE HUMMINGBIRD

NEARLY thirty years ago, I planted seven trees in Kenya. Those seven trees led to the creation of the Green Belt Movement. Since then, I have worked with women and men who have planted more than 30 million trees across Kenya, and we have shared our mission with many other countries in Africa.

Through the Green Belt Movement, thousands of communities, largely poor and rural, have been able to transcend ignorance and fear and take positive action for the earth. In the process, they have also secured their own livelihoods, as the trees provide them with fuel, fodder, protection against soil erosion, and even a small income.

One of the most important lessons I have learned is that all citizens need to be empowered. We need to feel that the life we want for ourselves and our children can be achieved only when we directly participate in protecting and restoring our environment. We can't wait for others to do it for us; we need to take action ourselves.

In Japan I learned the Buddhist word *mottainai.* It embraces the practice of not wasting resources and of using them with respect and gratitude. I have been sharing that word, *mottainai,* wherever I go because I think it's a beautiful word, and it also captures in one term the "three Rs" that environmentalists have been campaigning on for a number of years: reduce, reuse, and recycle. I am seeking to make *mottainai* a global campaign, adding one more "R" suggested by Klaus

Töpfer, the head of the United Nations Environment Program: "repair" resources where necessary. I have been consciously practicing the four Rs.

We can practice *mottainai* in rich countries where overconsumption is rampant, and we can also do it in regions where environmental devastation is causing the poor to get poorer and the ecosystems on which they depend to be degraded, some beyond repair.

In my case, *mottainai* means continuing to plant trees, particularly now that the long rains have come to Kenya. I have also called on my parliamentary colleagues to ensure that government offices use both sides of each sheet of paper so that we can halve the amount of paper we consume.

And I am urging the public and manufacturers not to use plastic bags that are so thin they tear almost immediately or are used once and thrown away. These bags clog waste dumps and blight the landscape in Kenya and around the world. They also provide good breeding grounds for disease-carrying mosquitoes.

If we did not use these bags, and instead carried our shopping in long-lasting and environmentally friendly containers such as kiondos and other baskets, we could revitalize traditional industries like basket and cloth weaving. This could become a global trend. If Kenya began exporting to developed countries at a fair price millions of kiondos woven by women from sustainably harvested sisal plants, that would be an important contribution to the protection of the earth, to rural livelihoods, and to fair trade.

We could also walk or use bicycles when we can, and avoid excessive use of airplanes.

These are just a few examples. There are many others relevant to your life, your community, and your country.

We sometimes underestimate what we can accomplish as individuals, but there is always something we can do. Like the little hummingbird in the story that follows, we must not allow ourselves to become overwhelmed, and we must not rest. This is what we are called to do. Today and every day, let us dedicate ourselves to making *mottainai* a reality. It is our human responsibility to appreciate nature and to preserve and protect the world's natural resources. We can all be like the hummingbird, doing the best we can.

FLIGHT OF THE

HUMMINGBIRD

Here is the story

OF THE GREAT FOREST

THAT CAUGHT ON FIRE.

The terrible fire raged and burned.

All of the animals were afraid and fled from their homes. The elephant and the tiger, the beaver and the bear all ran, and above them the birds flew in a panic.

They huddled at the edge of the forest and
watched. All of the creatures gathered, except one.

Only Dukdukdiya, the little hummingbird, would not abandon the forest. Dukdukdiya flew quickly to the stream. She picked up a single drop of water in her beak.

Dukdukdiya flew back and dropped the water on the fire.

Again she flew to the stream and brought back another drop, and so she continued—back and forth, back and forth.

The other animals watched Dukdukdiya's tiny body fly against the enormous fire, and they were frightened. They called out to the little hummingbird, warning her of the dangers of the smoke and the heat.

"What can I do?" sobbed the rabbit. "This fire is much too hot."

"There is too much smoke!" howled the wolf.

"My wings will burn! My beak is too small!"
cried the owl.

But the little hummingbird persisted. She flew
to and fro, picking up more water and dropping it,
bead by bead, onto the burning forest.

Finally, the big bear said, "Little Dukdukdiya,
what are you doing?"

Without stopping, Dukdukdiya looked down at all of the animals. She said, "I am doing what I can."

THE HUMMINGBIRD'S EFFECT

THIS story of a small, committed bird determined to put out a forest fire is inspired by a parable told by the Quechuan people of present-day Ecuador. The hummingbird is a frequent character in the stories of the indigenous peoples of the Americas, the exclusive home of more than 350 species of the extraordinary little bird.

The hummingbird often symbolizes beauty and agility, as well as optimism, wisdom, and the celebration of life. Spotting a hummingbird is usually cause for joy and a sign of good things to come. The Aztec deity Huitzilopochtli is often depicted as a hummingbird, and the Aztec people believed that dead warriors are reincarnated as hummingbirds. To the Chayma people of Trinidad, hummingbirds are dead ancestors, so there is a taboo against harming them.

The Mayan of Central America say the hummingbird is actually the sun in disguise, and he is trying to court his beloved, who is the moon. The Jatibonicu Taino Nation of Puerto Rico tells the tragic story of young lovers from rival families; their situation is memorialized when one becomes a hummingbird and the other a bright-red flower.

Fire, rain, and water are frequent elements in hummingbird stories. The hummingbird is said to have been born from fire, which explains its marvelous fiery feathers, while other stories suggest that it was the hummingbird who brought fire to the earth.

The Hopi and Zuni ask the hummingbirds to intervene on their behalf to persuade the gods to

bring rain. In thanks, these peoples often paint hummingbirds on their water jars. There is a parable from the Tarascan Nation of Mexico about a woman who is taught how to weave beautiful baskets by a grateful hummingbird to whom she had given sugar water during a drought.

The Pueblo Indians celebrate hummingbird dances and use hummingbird feathers in rituals to bring rain. One Pueblo story tells of a demon who is blinded after losing a bet with the sun. In anger he spews out hot lava and causes the earth to catch fire. A hummingbird gathers clouds from the four directions to bring rain, which puts out the flames. The bright colors on a hummingbird's throat remind us that he fled the fire through a rainbow.

The Mojave recount the pathfinding skills of this small creature. During a time when the people lived in an underground world of darkness, they sent a hummingbird to look for light. High above them, the bird found a path to the sunlit upper world where the people now live.

The Haida Nation of the North Pacific call the hummingbird *dukdukdiya,* in imitation of the small bird's voice. They tell the story of Haida explorers who had traveled offshore in a canoe for two months before discovering a peopled land where many bees and birds, including the hummingbird, lived in caves. For four years the travelers stayed in this land, but when the hummingbird flew out of the caves, the Haida also left and returned home.

As with Dukdukdiya in the burning forest and the hummingbirds that populate the stories and parables of many peoples, it's not necessarily the largest, most courageous, or loudest animal that can do the most good or have the greatest influence. Rather, those who are not afraid to act, and who are aware of what is at stake, can make the biggest difference.

Michelle Benjamin

Portions of this section are drawn from www.hummingbirdworld.com

His Holiness the Dalai Lama

UNIVERSAL

RESPONSIBILITY

S A BOY studying Buddhism, I was taught the importance of a caring attitude toward the environment. In Buddhism, our practice of non-violence and the ending of all suffering means that we become accustomed to not harming or destroying anything indiscriminately. Just as we should cultivate gentle and peaceful relations with our fellow human beings, we should also extend that attitude toward the natural environment. We share a sense of universal responsibility for both humankind and nature.

The survival of life on earth as we know it is threatened by human activities that lack a commitment to nonviolence and humanitarian values. The environment—the source of life for all beings in the world—continues to undergo extensive degeneration, and this destruction of nature and the earth's natural resources results from ignorance, greed, and lack of respect for the earth's living things. This lack of respect extends even to the earth's human descendants. These future generations will inherit a vastly degraded planet if destruction of the natural environment continues at the present rate.

Our ancestors viewed the earth as rich and bountiful, which it is. Many people in the past also saw nature as inexhaustibly sustainable, which we know is the case—but only if we care for it. We must consider future generations: a clean environment is a human right like any other. If we exploit the environment in extreme ways, even though we may get some money or other benefit from it now, in the long run we ourselves will suffer and future generations will suffer. It is therefore part of our responsibility toward others to ensure that the world we pass on is as healthy as when we found it, if not healthier.

Of course, when we say "us" or "humanity" or "society," it's obvious the initiative must come from individuals. Large human movements spring from individual human efforts. Yes, one individual can change the world! The problems resulting from our neglect of our natural environment are a powerful reminder that we all have a contribution to make. And while one person's actions alone may not have a significant impact, the combined effect of millions of individuals' actions certainly does. First, it is important to realize we are part of nature. Ultimately, nature will always be more powerful than human beings, even with all our nuclear weapons, scientific equipment, and knowledge. If the sun disappears or the earth's temperature changes by a few degrees, then we are really in trouble.

At a deeper level, we should recognize that although we are part of nature, we can control and

change things through our intelligence. Among
the thousands of species of mammals on earth, we
humans have the greatest capacity to alter nature.
As such, we have a twofold responsibility. Morally,
as beings of higher intelligence, we must care for this
world. The other inhabitants of the planet—insects
and hummingbirds and so on—do not have the
means to save or protect this world. Our other
responsibility is to undo the serious environmental
degradation that is the result of incorrect human
behavior. We have recklessly polluted the world with
chemicals and nuclear waste, selfishly consuming
many of its resources. Humanity—and every
individual within that—must take the initiative to
repair and protect the world.

In order to succeed in the protection and conservation of the natural environment, it is important
first of all to bring about an internal balance within
human beings themselves. The abuse of the environment arose out of ignorance. It is essential to help
people to understand this. I try always to express
the value of having a good heart. This simple aspect
of human nature can be nourished to great power.

With a good heart and wisdom you have the right motivation and will automatically do what needs to be done. If people begin to act with genuine compassion for everyone, we can still protect each other and the natural environment. This is much easier than having to adapt to the severe and incomprehensible environmental conditions projected for the future.

It is up to us as individuals to do what we can, however little that may be. Just because switching off the light when leaving a room seems inconsequential, it does not mean that we should not do it. Similarly, it is inappropriate to randomly discard fruit peels, paper, plastic bottles, old clothes, food leftovers and other kinds of garbage. Such things spoil the beauty of the landscape and are a hazard to health and hygiene.

Also, I have remarked on several occasions about the importance of tree planting. According to accounts of the Buddha's life, it would appear that he had a very deep relationship with nature and especially with trees. He was not born in the royal palace but in a park, under a sala tree. He attained complete enlightenment under the bodhi tree and left

this earth to enter nirvana between three sala trees. It would seem that the Buddha was very fond of trees.

Fortunately, the movement toward a deeper commitment to environmental protection through planting new trees and taking care of the existing ones is rapidly increasing all over the world. At a global level, trees and forests are closely linked with weather patterns and the maintenance of a crucial balance in nature. A healthy tree purifies the air and supplies oxygen for living beings to breathe. It harmonizes the elements and increases life expectancy. Its shade provides a refreshing place to rest. It nourishes crops and livestock and balances the temperature. It contributes to an attractive landscape and continually replenishes its surroundings.

I always stress the need to consider how our actions, in affecting the environment, are likely to affect others. I admit that this is very often difficult to judge. We cannot say for sure what the ultimate effects of, for example, deforestation might be on the soil and the local rainfall, let alone what the implications are for the planet's weather systems. The only clear thing is that we humans are the only species with the power to destroy the earth as we know it. The birds have no such power, nor do the insects, nor does any other mammal. Yet if we have the capacity to destroy the earth, so, too, do we have the capacity to protect it.

The key thing is a sense of universal responsibility; that is the real source of strength, the real source of happiness. If our generation exploits everything available—the trees, the water, and the minerals—without any care for the coming generations or the future, then we are at fault, aren't we? But if we have a genuine sense of universal responsibility as our central motivation, then our relations with our neighbors, both domestic and international, will improve.

This need for a sense of universal responsibility affects every aspect of modern life. Nowadays, significant events in one part of the world eventually affect the entire planet. Therefore, we have to treat each local problem as a global concern from the moment it begins. We can no longer invoke the national, racial, or ideological barriers that separate us without prompting destructive repercussions.

Whether we like it or not, we have been born on this earth as part of one great family. Rich or poor, educated or uneducated, belonging to one nation or ideology or another, ultimately each of us is just a human being like everyone else. Furthermore, each of us has the same right to pursue happiness and avoid suffering. When you recognize that all beings are equal in this respect, you automatically feel empathy and closeness for them.

Of course, this sort of compassion is, by nature, peaceful and gentle, but it is also very powerful. It is the true sign of inner strength. We do not need to become religious, nor do we need to believe in an ideology. In the context of our interdependence, considering the interests of others is clearly the best form of self-interest. All that is necessary is for each of us to develop our good human qualities.

We need to teach people that the environment has a direct bearing on our own benefit. We must teach people to understand the need for environmental protection. We must teach people that conservation directly aids our survival. Besides, the environment does not need fixing. It is our behavior in relation to it that needs to change. The air we breathe, the water we drink, the forests and oceans that sustain millions of different life forms, and the climatic patterns that govern our weather systems all transcend national boundaries. This is a source of hope. It means that no country, no matter either how rich and powerful or how poor and weak, can afford to not take action.

Ultimately, the decision to save the environment must come from the human heart. I want to tell you that self-confidence and enthusiasm are the keys to a successful life and to success in any activity one is engaged in. We must be determined and must have an optimistic outlook; then, even if we fail, we will have no regrets. Once you have made up your mind, you must go forward with a single-minded devotion in spite of the obstacles. This is very important.

Clearly this is a pivotal generation. Our beautiful world is facing many crises. It is not a time to pretend everything's good. Global communication is possible, yet confrontations take place more often than meaningful dialogues for peace. Our marvels of science and technology are matched, if not outweighed, by many current tragedies, including human starvation in some parts of the world and extinction of other life forms. Exploration of outer space takes place at the same time the earth's own oceans, seas, and fresh-water areas grow increasingly polluted, and their life forms are still largely unknown or misunderstood. Many of the earth's habitats, animals, plants, insects and even micro-organisms that we know as rare may not be known at all by future generations.

However, I feel optimistic about the future. The rapid changes in our attitude toward the earth are a source of hope. As recently as a decade ago, we thoughtlessly devoured the resources of the world as if there were no end to them. Now, both individuals and governments are seeking a new ecological and economic order. We have the capability and the responsibility. We must take into account that great love and great achievements involve great risk. We must act before it is too late.

Michael Nicoll Yahgulanaas

A SINGLE

BEAD OF WATER

F LIGHT is not exclusive to a single species, nor
is the ability to fly restricted to those with the
greatest wingspan. Just as many creatures—known
and unknown—can fly, the accomplishment of great
deeds is not the sole domain of the largest, the most
dominant, or even the most apparent. The tiniest
of notions can fly.

In Haida stories it is often the most diminutive creature—a mouse, a frog, or even that curious being that becomes smaller the closer it approaches—that offers the critical gift or the necessary solution. One of our foundational narratives describes a dark time when all the light in the universe is stored away inside the smallest container and is released only when the greatest hero becomes a small child. The wee creatures don't seek a lofty status, but their humble contributions, even a single bead of water, allow for heroic events.

Solutions to the numerous challenges in our lives are not usually delivered by a thousand warriors marching to a hundred drums and led by a grand general. Effective responses are often small and immediately appropriate—the acts that we as individuals are entirely capable of undertaking.

When we put away the notion that greatness is essential to success, then we expand into our full capacity. The hummingbird's faith in the power of the small, and in herself, is illustrated by her heroic contribution—the act of simply doing what she can, alone.

Imagine that many, most, or even all of the animals also did what they could. They might never know whether the problem was solved by their individual efforts, but their contribution would increase the likelihood that many beads of water would overcome the fire.

But that's another story.

Wangari Muta Maathai

WANGARI Muta Maathai was born in Nyeri, Kenya, in 1940, the daughter of farmers in the highlands of Mount Kenya. She is the founder of the Green Belt Movement, which through networks of rural women has planted over 30 million trees across Kenya since 1977. In 1986 the Movement established a Pan-African Green Belt Network that has taught people from other African countries about the Green Belt Movement's approach to environmental conservation and community building.

Several African countries have since started similar successful initiatives.

Wangari Maathai is internationally recognized for her persistent struggle for democracy, human rights, and environmental conservation. She has addressed the United Nations on several occasions, and she spoke on behalf of women at special sessions of the General Assembly for the five-year review of the 1992 Earth Summit. She has served on the United Nations Commission for Global Governance and co-chaired the Jubilee 2000 Africa Campaign. She and the Green Belt Movement have received numerous international awards, most notably the 2004 Nobel Peace Prize. Professor Maathai serves on the boards of several organizations, including the UN Secretary General's Advisory Board on Disarmament, the Women's Environment and Development Organization, World Learning (USA), Green Cross International, Environment Liaison Centre International, the WorldWIDE Network of Women in Environmental Work, and the National Council of Women of Kenya.

In 2002 Maathai was elected to Kenya's Parliament in the first free elections in a generation, and in 2003 she was appointed assistant minister for the environment. In 2005 she was elected presiding officer of the Economic, Social and Cultural Council of the African Union. Eleven African heads of state also appointed her a goodwill ambassador for the Congo Basin forest ecosystem, an advocacy role for the conservation and protection of this vital zone.

Professor Maathai is the mother of three children. She has published three books: *Unbowed: A Memoir, The Green Belt Movement: Sharing the Approach and the Experience,* and *The Canopy of Hope: My Life Campaigning for Africa, Women, and the Environment.* She lives and works in Nairobi.

Portions of this biography are drawn from www.wangarimaathai.com

His Holiness
the Fourteenth Dalai Lama

HIS HOLINESS the Fourteenth Dalai Lama, Tenzin Gyatso, is the head of state and the spiritual leader of the Tibetan people. He was born on July 6, 1935, to a farming family in a small hamlet in Taktser, northeastern Tibet. At the age of two, in accordance with Tibetan tradition, he was recognized as the reincarnation of his predecessor, the Thirteenth Dalai Lama.

His Holiness began his monastic education at the age of six. At twenty-three, in 1959, he sat his final examination in the Jokhang Temple, Lhasa, during the annual Monlam (Prayer) Festival. He passed with honors and was awarded the Geshe Lharampa degree, equivalent to a doctorate in Buddhist philosophy.

In 1950, after China's invasion of Tibet, the fifteen-year-old Dalai Lama was called upon to assume full political power. In 1954 he went to Beijing for peace talks with Mao Tse-tung and other Chinese leaders, but in 1959 he was forced to escape into exile. Since then he has been living in Dharamsala, northern India, the seat of the Tibetan political administration in exile and the home of many thousands of Tibetans in exile.

His Holiness is devoted to peace. In 1989 he was awarded the Nobel Peace Prize for his nonviolent struggle for the liberation of Tibet. He has consistently advocated policies of nonviolence, and he also became the first Nobel laureate to be recognized for his concern for global environmental problems.

The Dalai Lama has traveled to more than sixty-two countries spanning six continents. He has met with presidents, prime ministers, and rulers of major nations. He has held dialogues with the heads of many different religions and many well-known scientists. He has presented his message of peace and compassion to millions of followers worldwide and has introduced popular Buddhist concepts to the West.

Since 1959 His Holiness has received over eighty-four awards, honorary doctorates, and prizes in recognition of his message of peace, nonviolence, interreligious understanding, universal responsibility, and compassion. He has authored more than seventy-two books, many of them international best sellers. He describes himself as "a simple Buddhist monk."

Portions of this biography are drawn from www.dalailama.com

Michael Nicoll Yahgulanaas

MICHAEL Nicoll Yahgulanaas, an artist formally trained in Haida design, is translating this traditional indigenous iconography into contemporary signs. He has developed a new genre—Haida Manga—that reflects both his indigenous and colonial heritages and is influenced by his long and active career in social and environmental justice issues on his home islands of Haida Gwaii and throughout the Pacific Rim. His socially relevant work has been enthusiastically received in Japan and Korea and is published in Japan, Hong Kong, Taiwan, Macao, and Canada. He has exhibited in Asia and Europe and, most recently, in North America.

Michael's body of artistic works includes installation, sculpture, canvas, and paper, and in his words it features "an enthused and unusually joyful deflation of our serious selves." He lives in Canada and is currently working on a full-length Haida Manga book scheduled to be released in 2009.